Queen Conch

Test Pattern

PLATE 1

PLATE I

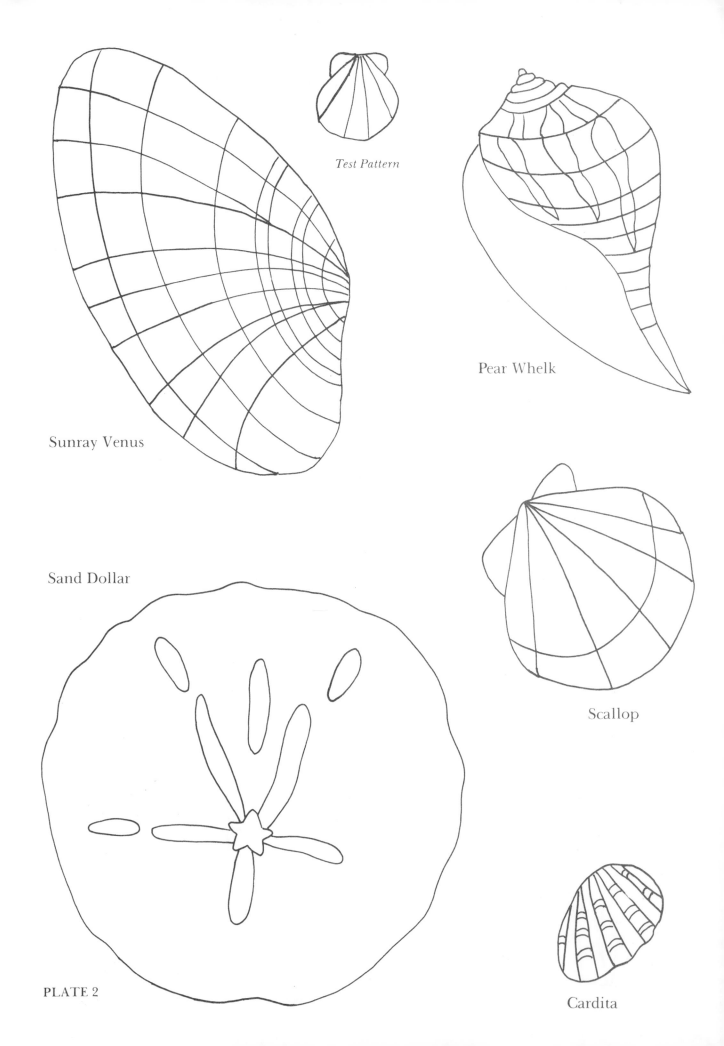

Test Pattern

Pear Whelk

Sunray Venus

Sand Dollar

Scallop

PLATE 2

Cardita

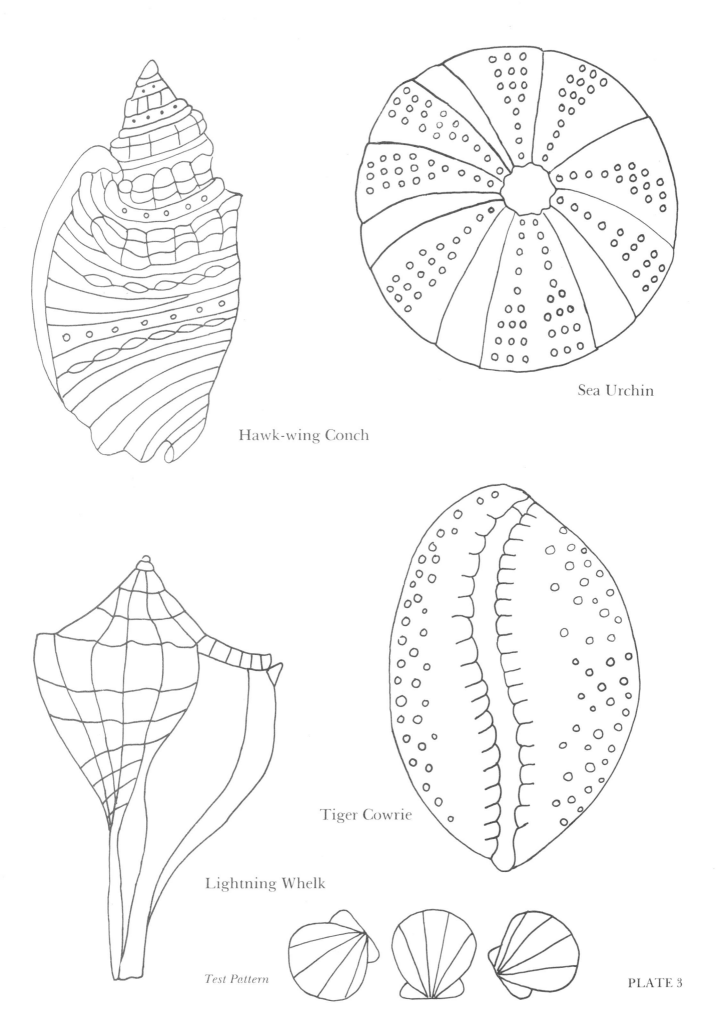

Hawk-wing Conch

Sea Urchin

Lightning Whelk

Tiger Cowrie

Test Pattern

PLATE 3

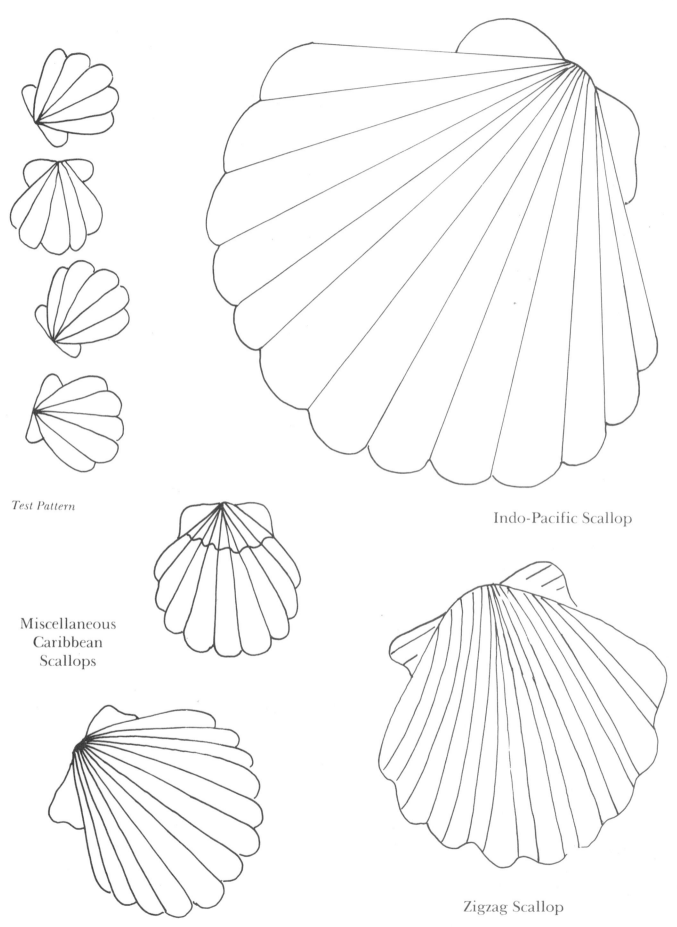

Test Pattern

Miscellaneous
Caribbean
Scallops

Indo-Pacific Scallop

Zigzag Scallop

PLATE 4

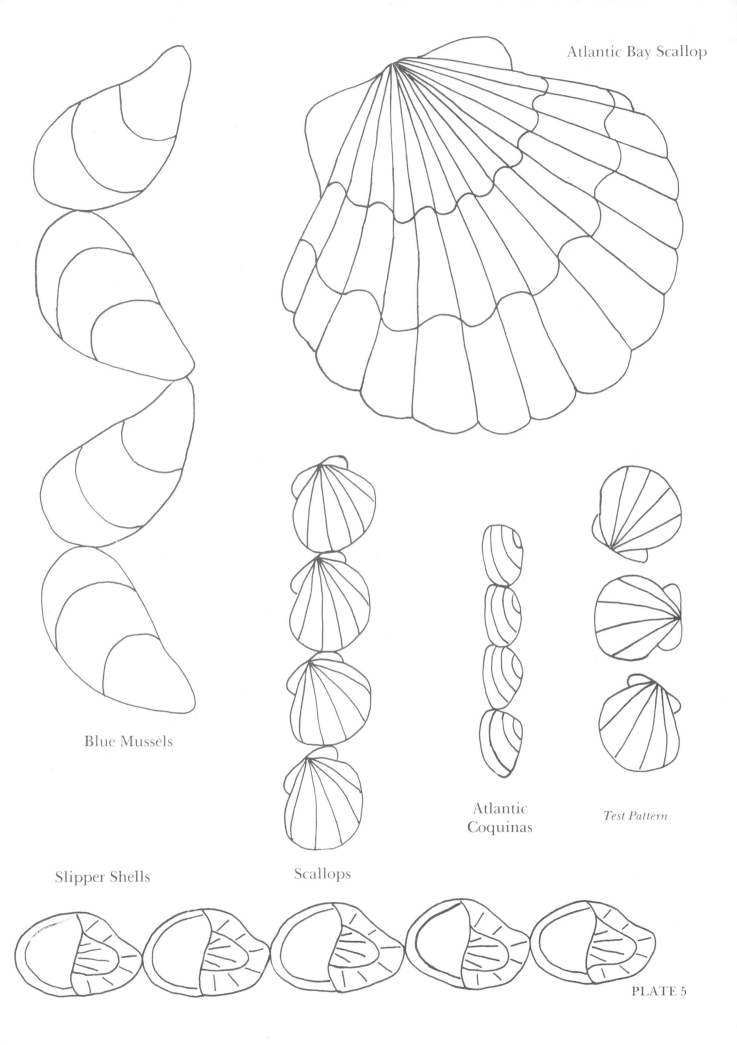

Atlantic Bay Scallop

Blue Mussels

Scallops

Atlantic Coquinas

Test Pattern

Slipper Shells

PLATE 5

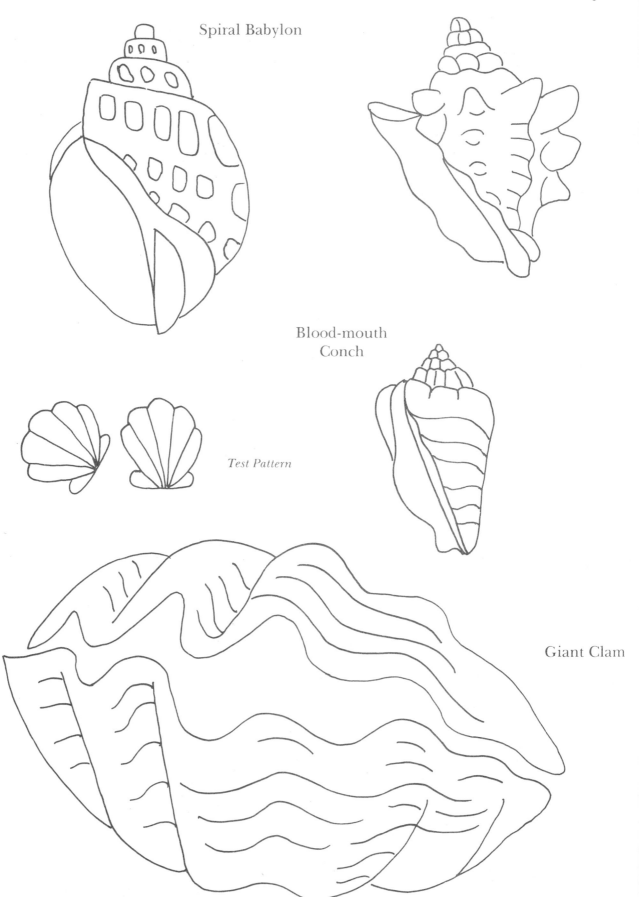

Spiral Babylon

Knobbed Purple

Blood-mouth Conch

Test Pattern

Giant Clam

PLATE 6

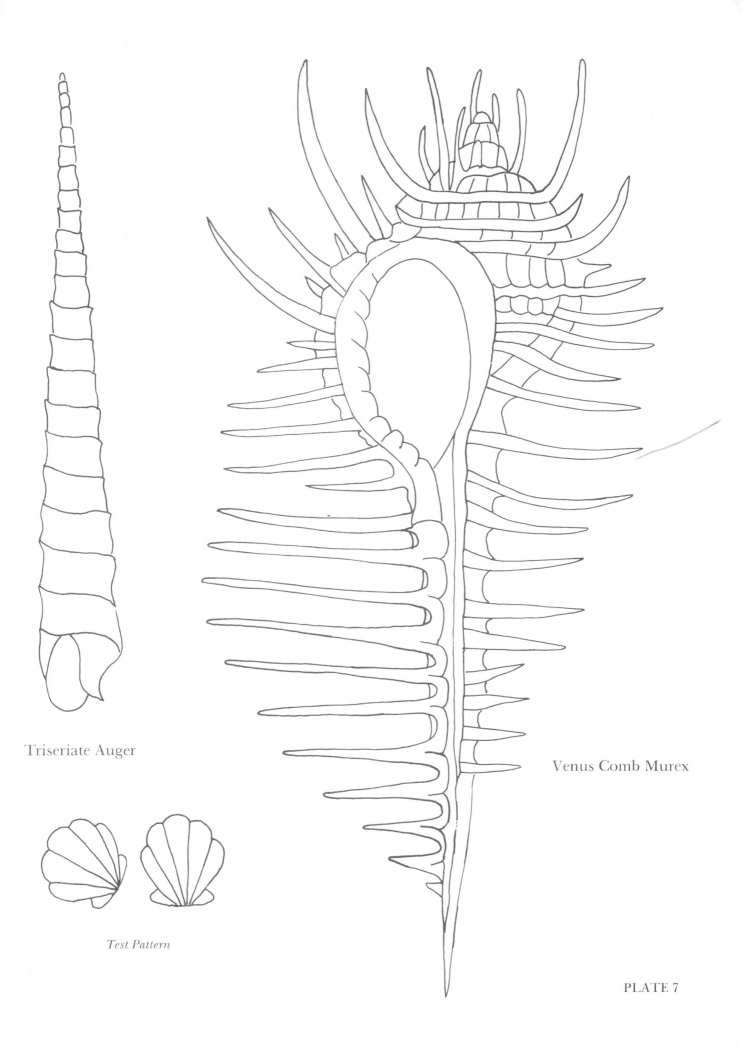

Triseriate Auger

Venus Comb Murex

Test Pattern

PLATE 7

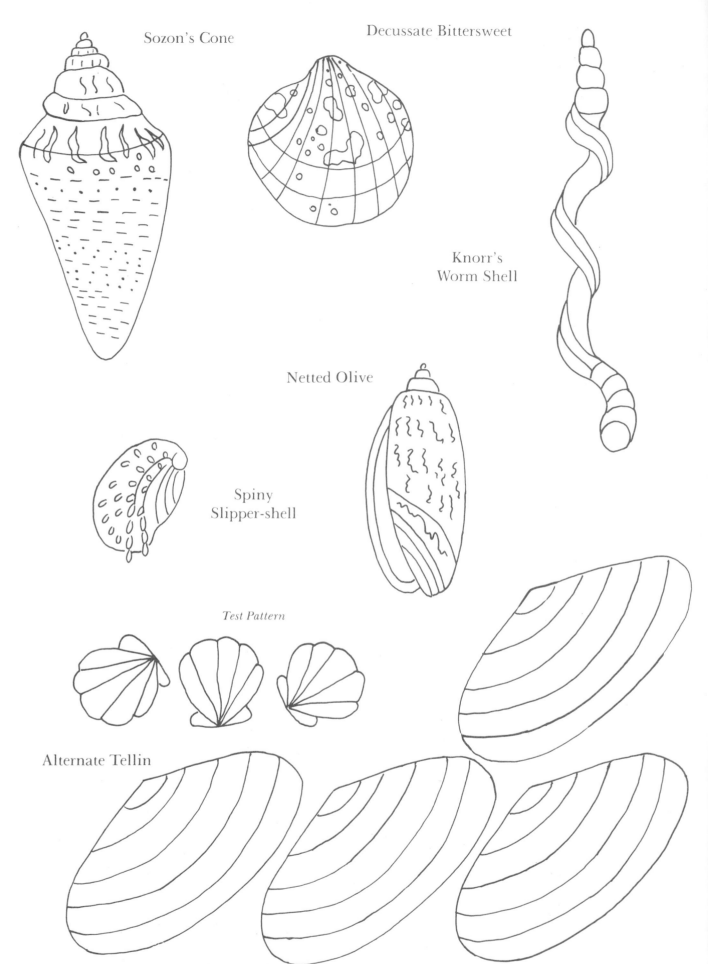

Sozon's Cone

Decussate Bittersweet

Knorr's
Worm Shell

Netted Olive

Spiny
Slipper-shell

Test Pattern

Alternate Tellin

PLATE 8

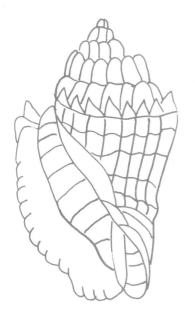

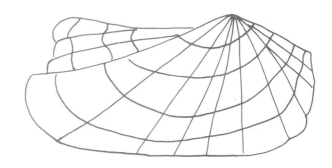

Turkey Wing

American Crown Conch

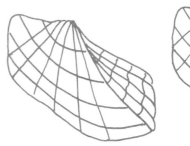

Mossy Ark

Caribbean Oyster

Buttercup
Lucina

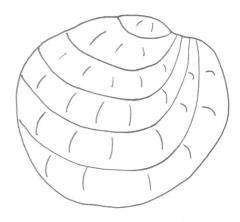

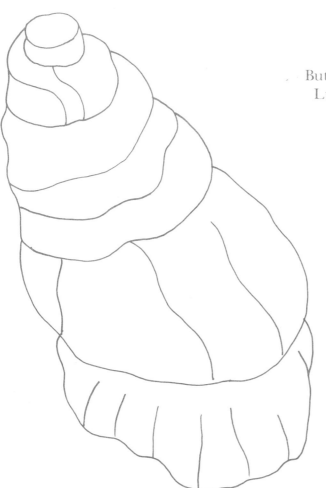

Test Pattern

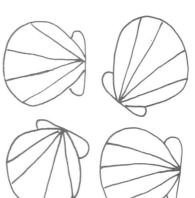

PLATE 9

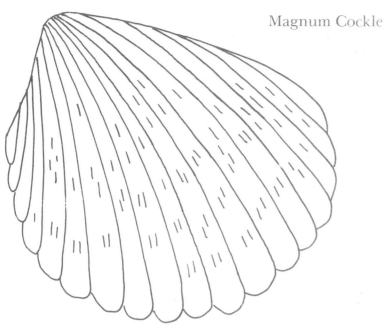

Magnum Cockle

Calico
Clam

Test Pattern

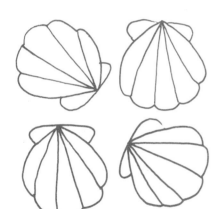

Pennsylvania Lucina

Southern Quahog

True Spiny Jewel Box

Cross-barred Venus

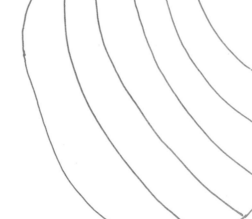

PLATE 10

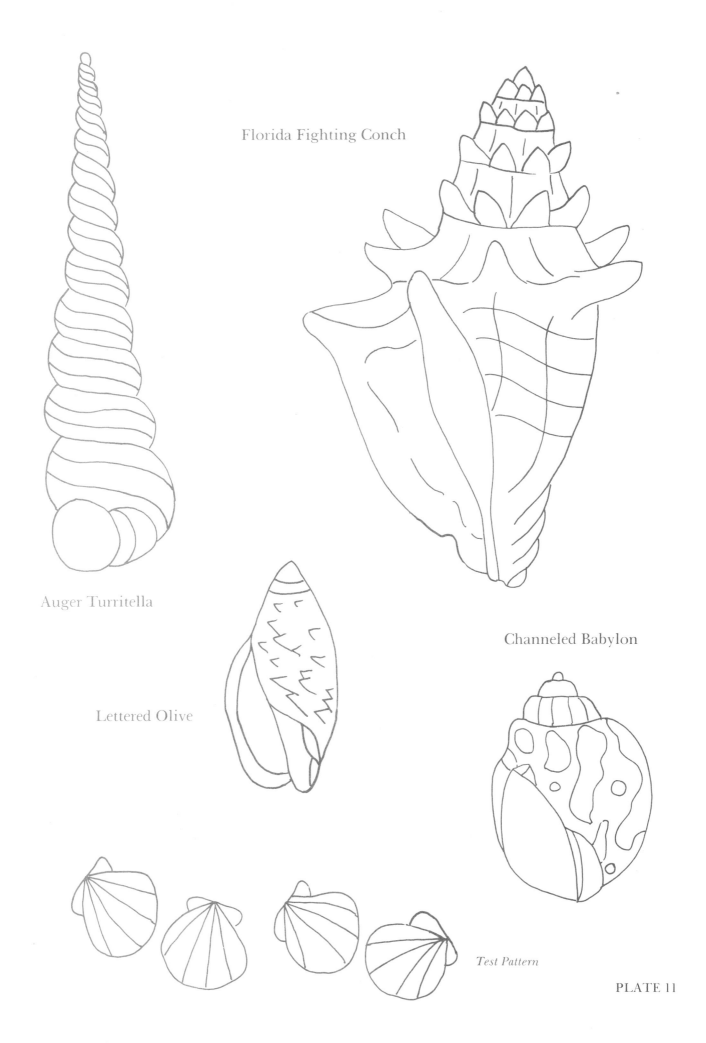

Florida Fighting Conch

Auger Turritella

Lettered Olive

Channeled Babylon

Test Pattern

PLATE 11

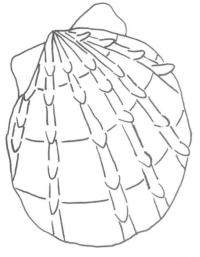

Kitten's Paw

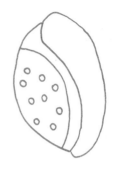

Bubble Shell

Atlantic Thorny Oyster

Atlantic Gray Cowrie

Limpet

Banded Tulip

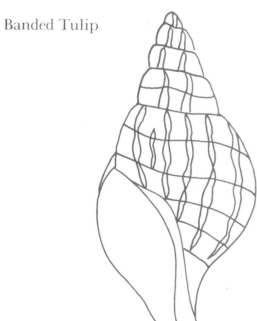

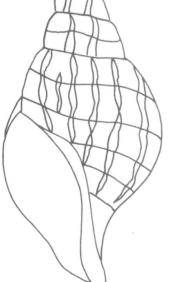

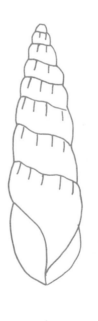

Cerith

Sunray Venus

Test Pattern

PLATE 12

Test Pattern

Chambered Nautilus

Blue Sea Star

Astrangia Coral

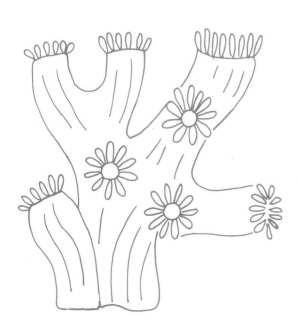

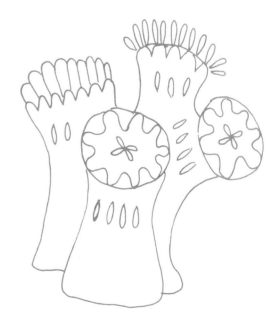

Rock
Barnacles

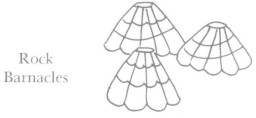

PLATE 13

Branching Coral

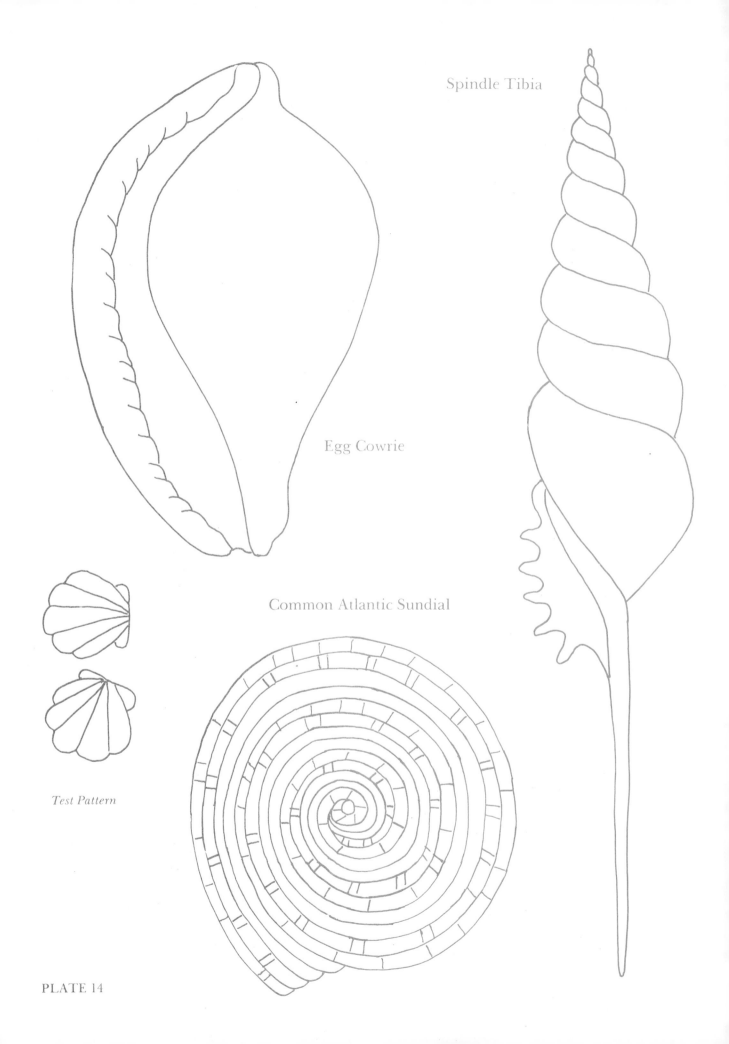

Spindle Tibia

Egg Cowrie

Common Atlantic Sundial

Test Pattern

PLATE 14

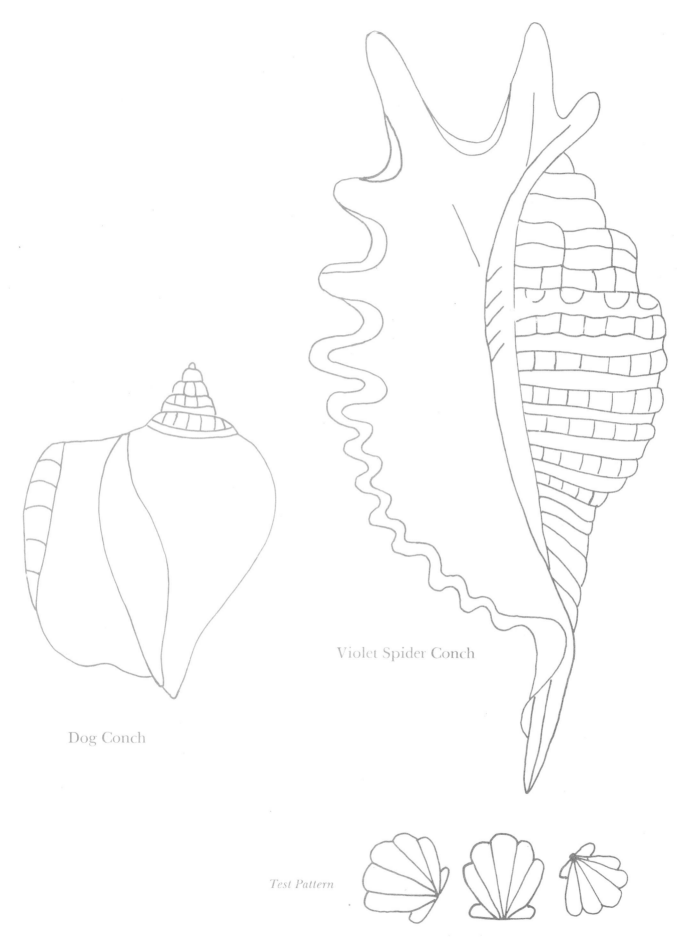

Dog Conch

Violet Spider Conch

Test Pattern

PLATE 15

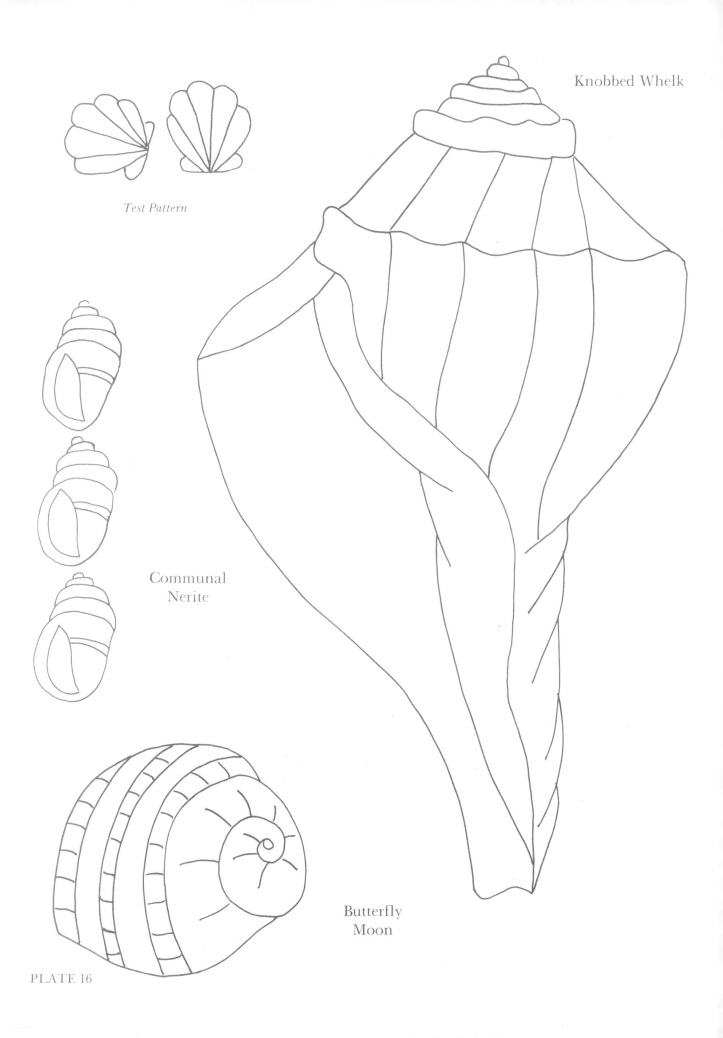

Knobbed Whelk

Test Pattern

Communal
Nerite

Butterfly
Moon

PLATE 16

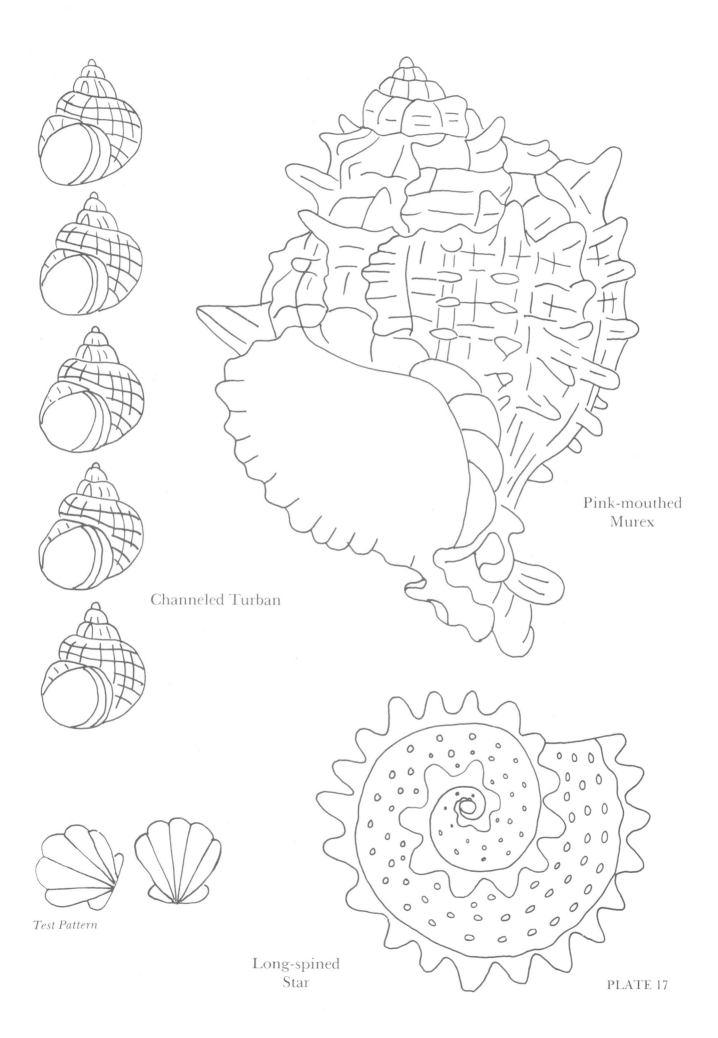

Pink-mouthed
Murex

Channeled Turban

Test Pattern

Long-spined
Star

PLATE 17

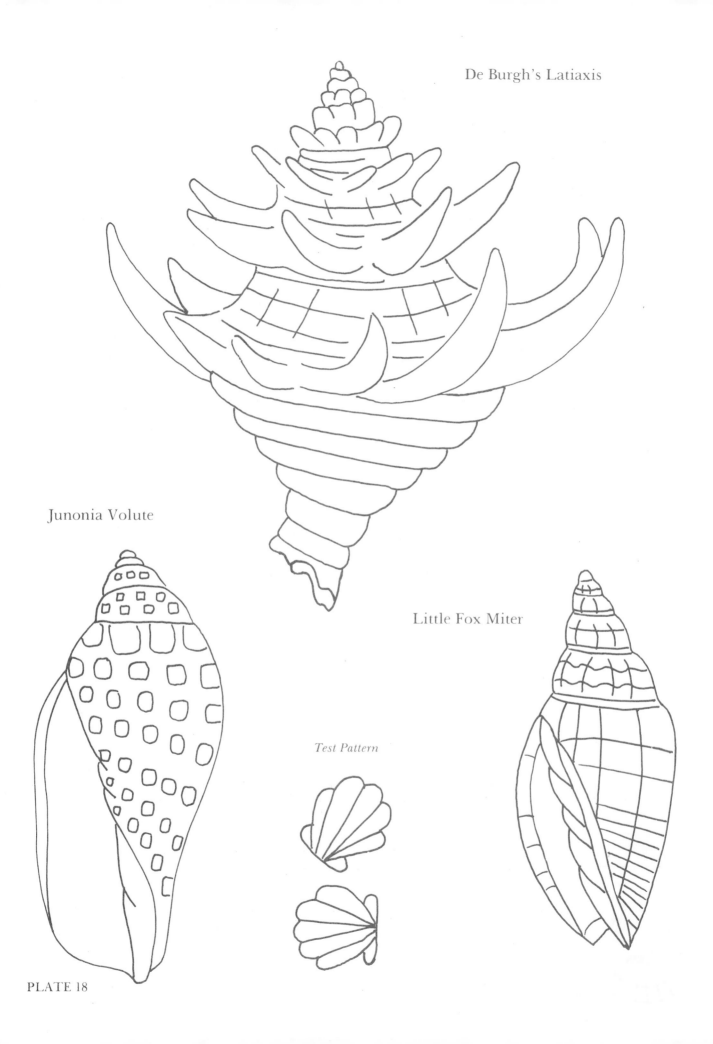

De Burgh's Latiaxis

Junonia Volute

Little Fox Miter

Test Pattern

PLATE 18

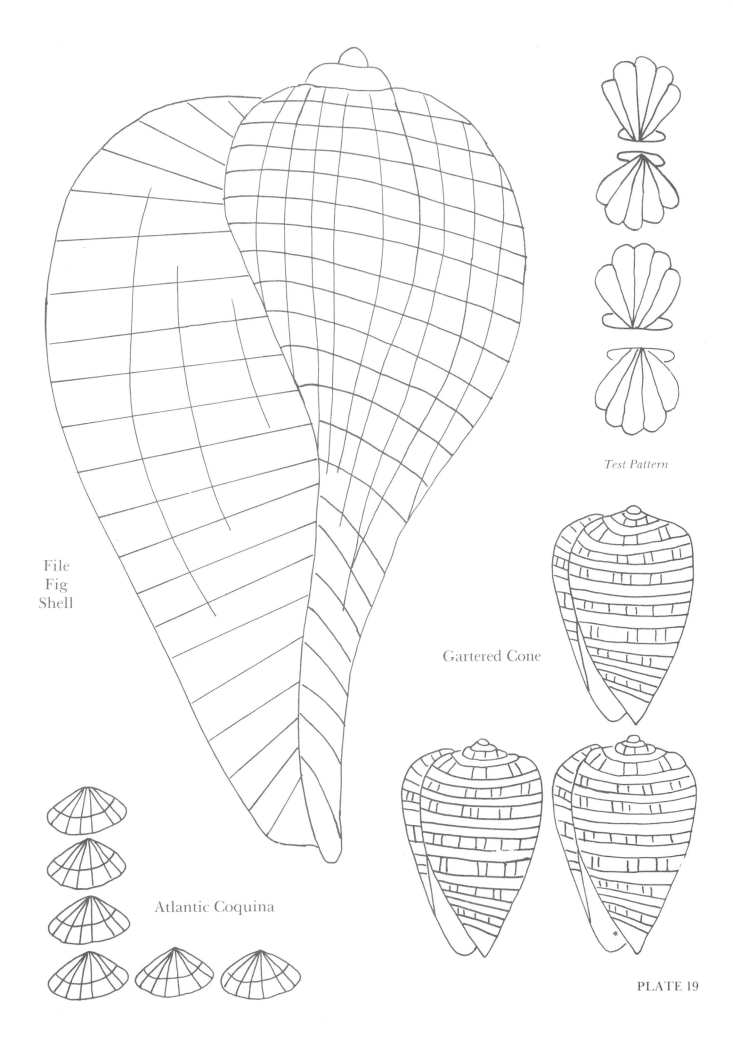

File
Fig
Shell

Test Pattern

Gartered Cone

Atlantic Coquina

PLATE 19

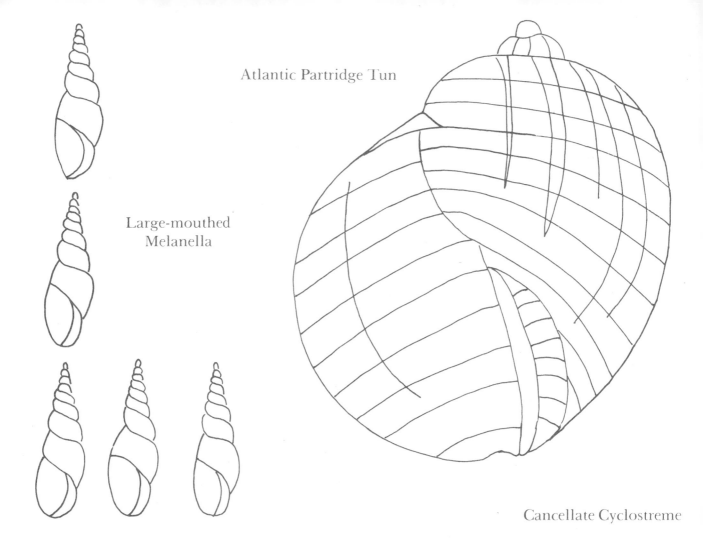

Atlantic Partridge Tun

Large-mouthed
Melanella

Cancellate Cyclostreme

Common Spirula

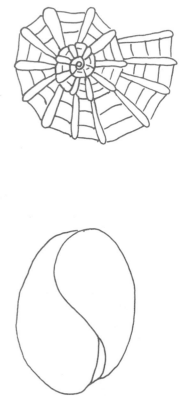

Test Pattern

Petit's Paper-bubble

PLATE 20

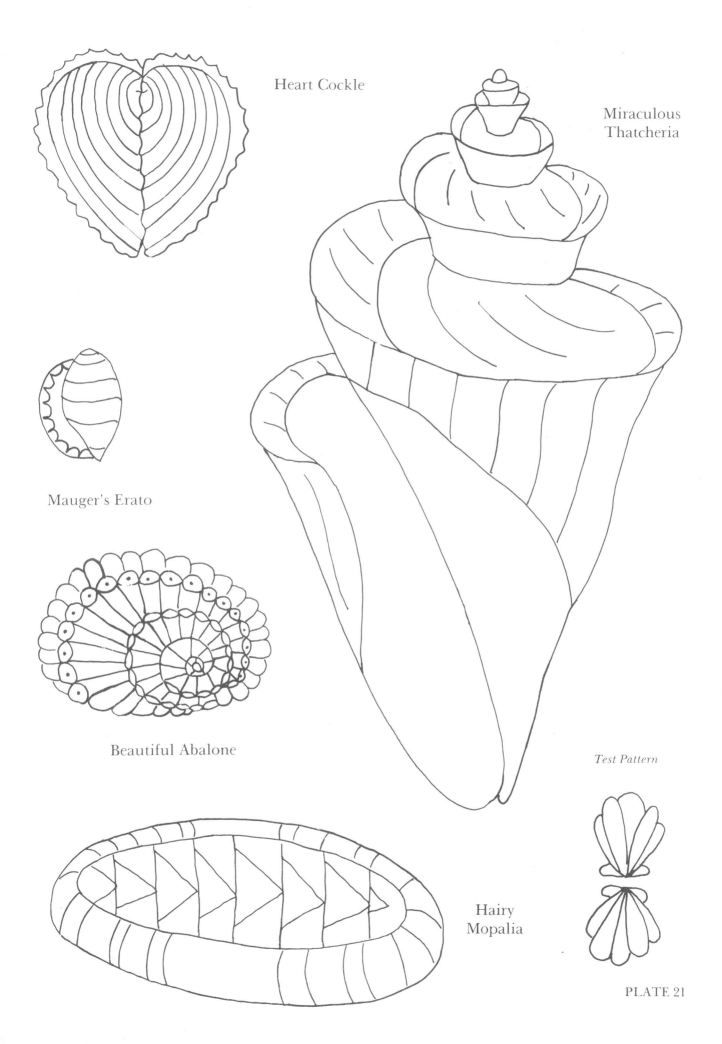

Heart Cockle

Miraculous
Thatcheria

Mauger's Erato

Beautiful Abalone

Test Pattern

Hairy
Mopalia

PLATE 21

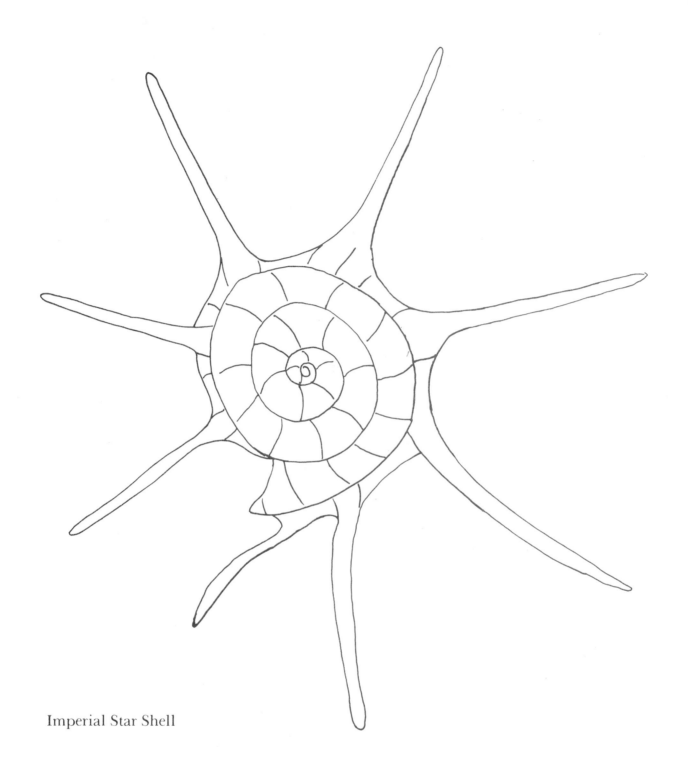

Imperial Star Shell

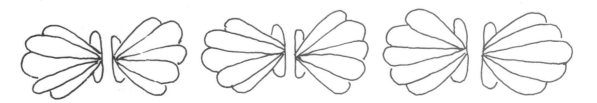

PLATE 22

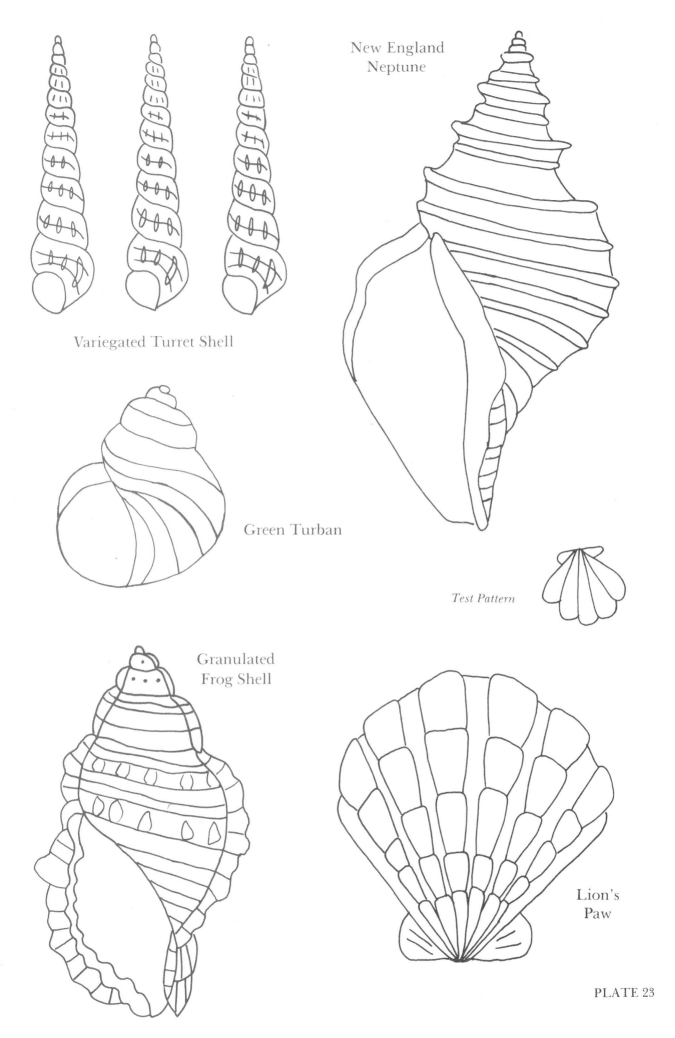

Variegated Turret Shell

New England
Neptune

Green Turban

Test Pattern

Granulated
Frog Shell

Lion's
Paw

PLATE 23

 Striated Bubble

 Common Cantharus

 Four-toothed Nerite

Middle-spined Cerith

 Milk Moon-shell

 Antillean Limpet

Atlantic Auger

 Atlantic Yellow Cowrie

 Gray Auger

Atlantic Modulus  Florida Cerith

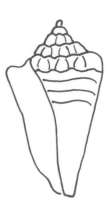

PLATE 24

Juvenile Milk Conch